Suddenly

SINGLE

A Guide For Rediscovering
Life After Tragic Loss

Suddenly
SINGLE

A Guide For Rediscovering
Life After Tragic Loss

For Sihnae.
With love + hope .
Ruthann

RUTHANN REIM McCAFFREE

LANGDON STREET PRESS

Langdon Street Press

212 3rd Avenue North, Suite 290

Minneapolis, MN 55401

612.455.2293

www.langdonstreetpress.com

ISBN-13: 978-1-936183-66-1

LCCN: 2011924461

Distributed by Itasca Books

Interior Design by Colleen Gray

Editing by Doreen Marchionni

Cover design by Tracey Reim Luckner (TraceyLuckner.com)

Author photograph by Joseph Boyle

Printed in the United States of America

Table of Contents

Introduction ix

My Story: A Sudden Ending 1

The Ten Survival Steps: Step One: Let Life Carry You. 7

Step Two: Say Goodbye 13

Step Three: Choose to Live 19

Step Four: Let Love In 23

Step Five: Learn to Answer the Question, "How *Are* You?" 29

Step Six: Accept the Truth. 35

Step Seven: Want More!. 41

Step Eight: Let Yourself Laugh 47

Step Nine: Face Forward and Take Back Your Power 51

Step Ten: Move Ahead With an Open Heart 57

A New Beginning. 63

From Surviving to Thriving: A Postscript. 73

Acknowledgments and Thanks 75

About the Author 78

Dedicated with love to Terry,

who always was

"one step ahead"

Introduction

For more than twenty-five years, I have counseled and coached hundreds of clients as they faced some of life's biggest challenges. I've admired their individual and collective strengths. Their resiliency, courage, and willingness to keep on keeping on have inspired me. Little did I know how much their examples of courage would sustain me as I faced my own biggest challenge.

When my husband of nearly forty years suddenly died from a fall at our home, I was catapulted into an aching transformation. Terry had always been bigger than life, and we had planned on living to 105. He was sixty-one, and we both thought he still had a lot of life in him. Besides, because I had married him so young, I didn't have a clue who I was without him. We were a team, and without him I suddenly found myself on the same challenging path that many of my clients had traveled. In the dark hours of the night and through the short, lonely days of my first winter alone, I recorded the story that you are about to read. It is a very personal journey meant as a gift to you.

But first, a bit about Terry. He was born in the heartland, where ripe, golden wheat waved in the wind, eight-man football brought out the whole town to cheer, and life was about the earth, the church, and hard work. But his roots in the tiny community of Marshall, Oklahoma, couldn't hold him. He wanted more, even after a college stint in Chicago. So he bought a red '57 Chevy convertible and drove west to the Pacific. He used to say that he came west to find his fortune and, in a way, he did. He found me, a redhead from California.

His love letters captured my heart—what a writer he was. (It's ironic that I'm the writer now, yet I know he would be proud.) The army soon found him and brought us to the Pacific Northwest, where he ultimately built one-of-a-kind houses and we built a family. The kid from Oklahoma loved boating in the salty waters of the Puget Sound, loved his family, and loved University Place, a wooded suburb near Tacoma, Washington, with sweeping, waterfront vistas. He picked this place to put down roots, dreamed the biggest dreams he could, and made them come true.

My story about losing him can't prescribe how you will go about the arduous task of putting your own life together after *your* sudden loss. Such a loss is huge because you have had no time to prepare. Mine is one person's experience. The rules for my life were suddenly new and the playing field different, but I found that many of the discoveries were parts of me I already knew. They were just waiting to be redis-covered. If my story restores your hope even a little, comforts you while you cry, makes you laugh, or gives you a new idea or two, I will feel that I have done my job. In my work I have always felt that the right people somehow find me, so if you have found me, I'm grate-ful to share this journey with you. I can tell you from my heart that even in the most difficult parts of this time, winter doesn't last forever, spring and even summer will come again, and your life will find its new beginning, too.

My Story: A Sudden Ending

In the Northwest, days of bright sunshine and clear skies are rare, and April 15, 2003, was one of the most beautiful of rare days. We woke early with the sun already shining, ready to walk. Our hiking boots tugged on, we climbed into Terry's car to drive to the top of the hill where we would take off on our two-mile trek. We teased each other that driving up the hill to walk was like eating low-fat frozen yogurt covered in chocolate, but the trip starts straight up, so we drove there. As we walked, we talked about a dream Terry had that morning that I'm still trying to understand. In it he was in Oklahoma on the farm where he grew up. A beautiful, sleek silver airplane landed on the dirt road on the east side of the farm. He ran for the plane, believing he was supposed to get aboard, and I thought he was going to tell me what happened when he climbed inside. Instead, he said that just as he reached the plane, it took off without him. Then he woke up.

Later, after our walk, I remember kissing him goodbye. We went on a romantic getaway over Valentine's Day and came home deciding to "put the bedroom through college" now that our children, Tracey and Brandon, were both grown and graduated. So on this day in April, our bedroom was a mess of construction, with no furniture or carpet, a new door, a new outside wall, and a soon-to-be new fireplace. We were sleeping in Tracey's room with Bogey and Katey, our two Norwegian forest cats, corralled to keep them from escaping through open construction doors. Terry slid Tracey's door open a crack and said, "I'm leaving. I'll see you tonight." He gave me a smack on the lips, I said "OK," and he was gone.

At about 1:30 that afternoon I had a few minutes before my next client. It seemed like the perfect time to slip out to the post office. In the parking lot sat Brandon's Honda Insight, which Terry had just driven back from Los Angeles for me to try out. I folded myself into its tiny front seat and eased out onto the street. All the new dials and instruments had my attention until I caught sight of a truck behind me with its lights flashing and the driver waving for me to pull over. It looked like Terry's old farm truck, but I didn't recognize the driver. "What in the world could this be about?" I wondered as I pulled into a drugstore parking lot. It turned out to be Terry's new handyman, whom I didn't know, rushing over out of breath and yelling, "Terry fell! Terry fell! Do you want me to take you to the hospital?" At this point I had no idea who this fellow was nor any real indication of how seriously Terry had been injured. Nor was I about to get into a car with someone I didn't know. I'm independent, and I figured I could manage.

I drove back to the office, tried unsuccessfully to call my client, and then left him a note on the door. I climbed back into that little car and headed out. After three blocks, my accelerator foot lost its push. Again, I pulled into the drugstore parking lot. What in the world was happening? My body was beginning to tell me what my heart and spirit couldn't understand.

What I did know was that I needed help. There was only one person to call, Terry's best pal and soulmate, Dixie, who worked just up the street. As luck would have it, she had just walked in the door. I don't remember what I said, but her answer was, "Don't leave. I'm on my way."

I climbed into her car and we saw an ambulance go by. We knew immediately Terry was in it, so Dixie pulled out of the parking lot like a shot. Though we were right behind the ambulance for half a mile, I couldn't see what was happening inside. Mostly I was aware of the flashing red lights and the sound of the siren. At the first big intersection, the ambulance went through a red light, and we were tempted to do the same, but good sense prevailed. However, we lost sight of the ambulance. The handyman had told me where they were taking Terry, but I couldn't remember. "Call the city offices," Dixie said. She knew someone there could call the fire station and find out where the ambulance was going. I called the office, and I heard someone talking to the dispatcher at the fire station on another line. When it appeared they weren't going to give us the location, Dixie yelled, "Dammit, my brother is a fireman, and I know they can contact that ambulance and find out where they're going!" That got results. The ambulance was heading to a Tacoma trauma center, and finally, so were we.

We rushed into the emergency room just as they were wheeling Terry off for either a CAT scan or an MRI, and I yelled, "That's my husband!" The trauma specialist introduced herself to me as they were moving Terry out of sight and said she'd be back as soon as possible to let us know what was going on. Someone in the ER gently took us to one side and introduced us to the on-call social worker, who led us to a small room off the larger waiting room. As we walked toward the smaller room, I looked back at the waiting room full of people. They didn't seem to have a social worker leading them to a private room. We were getting special treatment. This was not good. Usually my feelings rise to the surface easily and guide me through tough situations. About now they went into hiding with my heart, and my rational brain took over.

The handyman found us, and he handed me Terry's wallet and cell phone. As I stood clutching the wallet, I remembered it was April 15, tax day. We never got our taxes in early because money was always tight, and I guessed that maybe one reason Terry hadn't been careful going down that ladder was because he was thinking about getting to the bank. He had a big check to write to the IRS, and it had to go out that day. I looked in his wallet. There was my business check for half of the taxes and there was a blank check from his business account. I'm an honest person, but I wrote a check on his business account that I was pretty sure would be hot until I could make it right with the bank. My only thought was to get those checks in the mail. I called our accountant's office, and she sent a runner to the ER to pick up our checks to mail them out.

The doctor came in and the social worker stood near me as the doctor explained, "Terry had a very bad fall. It might not be survivable." Then the doctor left, and I turned to the social worker, saying, "My life is never going to be the same, is it?" "No," she said, "it's not." Then she said, "Call the kids. They have to come right away."

So I started making phone calls to alert the world that Terry—husband, son, dad, grandpa, best friend, community leader, leader of us all—was in trouble. Things were starting to happen and we still hadn't seen him. He was in the intensive-care unit in the last room, hooked up to all kinds of monitors and machines. Dixie and I had to walk the length of that unit to reach him, and my first thought when I saw him was, "He's already gone." Even though his hand was warm when I took it in mine and his chest was going up and down with breath, the essential "him" was just not there. I believe his spirit had left when he hit the ground at home and the rest of this was just to buy us a little time to get used to the shock. I leaned over to his right ear and whispered, "Honey, it's OK if you need to go. I'll be all right." The words came out of my mouth, but I didn't have a clue if they were true or what they were going to really mean. I just knew that if he needed to go, I needed to let him.

I remember Dixie and myself sitting, standing, sitting, standing, and asking the ICU nurses questions, all the time knowing in my heart that there was nothing for me to do in this room. What needed to be done was to go home and create a little order out of the chaos of the construction mess, because people would be coming. We needed beds with sheets and towels for bathing, and someone needed to vacuum up the cat hair. I wasn't surprised to be thinking about getting organized. When stress overwhelms me, my hands get busy cleaning. Terry used to tease me that we had the cleanest countertops in the county.

How could I return to that house where Terry was hurt? It was my home, and yet it hadn't kept my best friend safe. Going home was my first act of courage. "Oh my God, look at the gutter!" I cried when I rounded the corner by the garage. "It's been pulled loose from the house. Oh no, that's where he fell." He'd been up and down that same ladder in that same place hundreds of times. It wasn't raining. How could he have fallen? The handyman was on the roof with Terry at the time. Apparently they were talking about cleaning the gutters, and Terry was showing him what needed to be done. As the fellow turned back to grab a broom, Terry started down the ladder. He was always in too much of a hurry and distracted. It looked as though he grabbed the gutter to keep the ladder from falling, but the nails didn't hold, and he fell straight back onto the concrete walkway. If he had fallen just a foot to either side, he would have gone into flowerbeds. Apparently the handyman jumped down from the roof, gave Terry CPR, called 911, and watched the paramedics work on him until they were able to get him breathing again. Then he came looking for me. Much later I reflected on how much of a gift it was to know that Terry didn't fall alone, and that I didn't have to come home and find him on the concrete.

Once back in the house that day, I looked at the south wall of the bedroom and saw the new fireplace the work crew had just put in. I don't think Terry got to see it, but he would have been pleased. It was perfect, and yet it was so disconnected from what was really happening. We had a new, romantic fireplace, but my lover would never get to enjoy it.

By 10 p.m. the house was somewhat in order, so Dixie and I headed back to the hospital. Had we remembered to eat? It hadn't even crossed our minds. So we stopped in at a restaurant and found a quiet booth in a corner. I couldn't say what we ate, but I remember having a beer and how cold it felt going down. Trauma does strange things to memory. Some parts of that day will be with me until I die, while other parts disappeared as soon as they happened.

Back at the hospital Terry's situation hadn't changed. I still believed he was gone and that now we were just waiting for people to see him one last time. But before we could let him go, doctors needed to perform two tests to measure his brain pressure. Someone told me that if by some miracle he lived, he'd be in a nursing home for the rest of his life, because the swelling in his brain was creating pressure 300 percent above normal. "Oh no, Terry would hate that!" I said. The tests were conclusive, and we now had official word that our leader was gone.

Tracey was flying in from New Jersey, and I was waiting for a phone call from Brandon. The hard part of telling people was about to begin. Word was getting out, though. The flag by our town hall would be lowered to half-mast later that day, and a newspaper reporter would call. We were still at the hospital when someone asked if Terry had wanted to be an organ donor. He and I never talked about that. Because he was an accident victim, he was a donor candidate, but what were his wishes? Fortunately, the answer was on his driver's license, and I'll be forever grateful for that. So, we began to talk about what to donate. Organs, yes. Bones, yes. Eyes, yes. But not skin, I said, and I don't want his body going to science. There has to be something left to love.

I didn't know when we put him on life support that the medication affected his heart, lungs, and pancreas in such a way that they could not be transplanted. I am sad that his heart couldn't go to someone, because he had such a kind and generous one. I guess it was meant to stay with our family. And I wish the best for the people who got his eyes. He wore glasses from the time he was eight, and they were as thick as Coke bottles. But they saw beauty and possibility in the world, so that has to count for a lot.

He was gone, just like that. In the morning we were a couple, getting ready for a hectic, full day. By nightfall I was—what was I? Numb, in a daze, grateful for things to do, alone.

"The Ten Survival Steps"
Step One: Let Life Carry You

Going home from the hospital again was so weird. It was a day of stunning sunshine, and all the people Terry loved were starting to arrive. Our neighbor picked up Tracey at Seattle-Tacoma International Airport, and Brandon arrived a little later. Normally Terry was the one who made a gathering happen. He planned the food, shopped, and cooked, while I got the house ready. Well, the house was mostly ready, but none of us knew how we would make it without him. Who would organize the food, delegate the jobs, and keep things moving? Somehow food came and was served and eaten, and I don't have a clue how. All I knew was that people were unbelievably kind and generous. Over and over it left me stunned. Some say that when life is at its worst, human beings are at their best, and now I know that's true. For me it was like taking in night and day all at once, and it was only beginning. But loved ones, and I suppose life, carried me onward. Two especially close friends had left to go biking in Spain just days before Terry died. I remember asking them shortly before they left if they had a way to check e-mail, and they said they didn't. Somehow we found out how to reach them, and I told them what happened.

But before I could breathe normally, I was waiting for Bill, one of Terry's best friends, to arrive. He lives on the big island of Hawaii, and because it was both spring break and Easter, it was almost impossible for him and his wife to get a flight out. But I knew when they finally arrived everything would be OK. They're family of our hearts and knew what needed to be done and what Terry would have wanted. When they arrived three days later, I started to breathe more easily and move forward. The first thing Bill did was go through Terry's CDs, compiling thirty-five songs onto two CDs that gave us a collection of Terry's favorites. We ended up using the CDs for Terry's memorial, and I have listened to them hundreds of times. At first I cried every time I played them. Now, I mostly enjoy them because they are my favorites, too.

The arrangements

Eight of us went to the funeral home to make the arrangements for Terry's cremation. I'm a believer in inclusion, so everyone who wanted to come was invited. We walked in en masse and had to use a conference room because there were so many of us. On the way to the room, we walked by the business offices, and I swear I looked up and saw the words "sell, sell, sell" on the wall. It struck me as funny and I started to laugh. It reminded me of the embarrassing time Terry had said, "Here comes the body," during communion at a new church, and I burst out laughing. We bought everything we needed, and no one pressured us. I've since wondered if I really saw those words or if Terry just wanted us to laugh a little on such a sad mission.

We put on just the kind of celebration Terry would have loved. We used the CDs Bill assembled. Terry's mom and my mom searched through hundreds of pictures, which relatives scanned into the computer. Bless them, too. It took hours to put the PowerPoint presentation together, but everyone pitched in. Tracey wrote the obituary, and she and Brandon wrote the text for the memorial service. Our cousin arranged for the celebration to be filmed for Terry's dad because he was too ill to travel. Because Terry embraced the motto "shop local," we held the gathering at an almost local golf club. He didn't like golf, but we figured he could be a little flexible, and the place was wonderful.

SURVIVAL TIP

Look for opportunities to say yes to things that bring you joy.

About four hundred people came: family, friends old and new, business associates, city employees and council members, friends from our Rotary Club, former employees, and people who knew Terry through his many interests. When it was time to share memories and thoughts, dozens of people spoke, and we laughed and cried at the stories. Then we ate, just as we'd do at any great party. Terry had to feel loved and celebrated because that's what we were doing: loving and celebrating him.

Looking back, I'm amazed at how many people Terry saw the last few months of his life. He visited with both Tracey and Brandon, even though they live on opposite corners of the country from us. We had one grandchild at the time, Ben, who is Tracey and Steve's son and was born just seven months before Terry died. A week before the accident, Terry saw Ben because we heard he was eating bananas, and "Grandpa T" didn't want to miss a thing. Terry was proud that he had gotten to feed Ben and had even changed a poopy diaper. It was one more of those things he did in the last few months of his life that makes me believe somehow a person's spirit knows life is nearing an end, even if it doesn't make sense any other way. Terry loved Ben so much, and surely that love continues to this day.

Terry also untangled half a dozen nasty situations that would have left me reeling, including the taxes. And we had many chance conversations that continued to give guidance as we all struggled to figure out how to move forward. I remembered telling Terry, "I get to die first. How in the world would I ever deal with all of your business properties and clients?" His answer liberated me when I recalled it days after he died: "You'd be just fine. You won't do things the same way I do them and that's OK." Bill also recalled Terry had told him in February that he was going to Hanalei Bay in the summer to see the boats near the island of Kauai. It had long been the place we thought of as the most beautiful and sacred on earth, so it was natural to think of Terry wanting to go there. But we had mostly gone around Christmas to escape the dismal Northwest weather. When Bill remembered that conversation, it was clear that some of Terry's ashes would be going to Hanalei that summer.

Terry was cremated on the same day as his memorial service. His ashes came to me in a copper urn in honor of the copper cooking pots he used to create his famous meals. The funeral home had placed his urn in a small blue plastic carrying case with a handle, because I had explained we would eventually be traveling to Kauai. Again, it seemed unreal to be bringing my husband home in a suitcase when just days before we were tearing out the walls of our bedroom. I opened the case when I got home and carefully lifted out the urn. Then I placed it on the fireplace hearth by his photo and a basket that would eventually overflow with sympathy cards and memory letters. Later we would travel, but for awhile, he was home again with me.

Back to reality

Reality set in when I trekked to our attorney's office to read the will Terry and I wrote less than two years before. I faced a mountain of decisions, with a timeline and protections to follow that our complicated world made necessary. It was my first jump into the deep end of the pool. Fortunately, I had a team of loyal, professional advisers who were willing to jump in with me.

SURVIVAL TIP

Find skilled people you trust who will help you.

Work, as it turned out, was a haven, a place to go with real purpose and an opportunity to get out of the new life and back to something familiar. I returned to work three weeks after Terry died, and I'm still not sure how I rescheduled my missed clients' visits. But they welcomed me back, and we started rebuilding lives, theirs and mine. Another reality check was the realization that my two children were all grown up. When Tracey and Brandon were in college, I remember one of them protesting whenever I slipped and called them "the kids." Sometime later they relented and no longer resisted when I called them that. Now Tracey is married and has a son and daughter. Brandon is happy supporting the movie industry with his time and talent. These grown-up kids are strong and brave. Brandon was able to stay with me for two weeks after everyone else left, and I don't know what I would have done without his quiet courage and willingness to help me manage the stuff of life—cooking, eating, answering the telephone, bringing in the mail.

One of the sturdiest gifts he gave me was help with a three-year-long project due to culminate in May, just two weeks after Terry died. I called it "In Celebration of Women 2003," and *it* carried me because I certainly wasn't in any shape to carry *it*. Later, Brandon said it was my first act of courage, but I think it was life's willingness to show me

What and who gives you energy? Get more of it and them.

even in those dark early days that I was still alive and had something to offer.

The celebration started with a visit to the Annie Leibovitz photography exhibit Women, which toured the Pacific Northwest. Terry walked through the exhibit with me and held my hand as I cried at the strength of the women and the beauty of the ten-by-ten-foot photographs. Later, over several glasses of wine at a small café, I asked Terry, "Why can't I photograph the women in our small town who aren't famous but who are making a difference just because of who they are?" "Well, why can't you? What's stopping you?" he countered. "I'm a career counselor, not a photographer," I threw back. Nothing happened for two years, but like all good ideas, it patiently waited for me to bring it to life as a requirement for my professional coaching certification.

Surround yourself with beauty in whatever form you choose.

Terry was excited about what I was doing, and I was depending on him to help me pull the final event together. He was always so good about making things happen. This time it would have to happen without him, and frankly, I thought about just not doing it. But that just wasn't the answer. It was my first opportunity to say "yes" to life, so Brandon and I went ahead. Without him and good friends pitching in, there wouldn't have been a celebration. But on May 2, 2003, more than one hundred friends, family members, and community and business leaders gathered to honor fourteen women who make our small town better just because of who they are. My tears waited to fall until it was over.

Questions to ask yourself as you let life carry you:

1. What plans might you be tempted to put on hold that you could still carry out?

2. Who are the people you want to be around?

3. What is the best use of your energy?

4. What kind of physical movement can you engage in?

Step Two: Say Goodbye

Goodbyes come in colors, and I wished mine to Terry could have been a bright and beautiful rainbow. But at first it wasn't any color at all. We did have a quick kiss that morning and a "Have a good day. I'll see you tonight." But it wasn't, "Do you know how much I love you? Do you know how important you are to me and to this world? Do you know all the things that you have done to make your life so amazing? But you said you would live to be 105. You're not even close to that. We're not done. We have a new grandson. He needs to know you. I need to grow old with you. You can have your boat. Just don't go! Don't go. Please don't go now."

I've heard of people on the brink of death willed back to life by the call of their loved ones. My instinct would have been to try that. He loved life and I loved life with him. But he was gone before I got to him.

At first, I just kept wondering whether Terry was all right wherever he was. I'm spiritual, though not religious, and in my heart I believed he was just fine. But he was not even close to having spirit as his center, so I didn't really know. Maybe his beliefs put him in some kind of limbo land. Brandon and I walked our local labyrinth, a place of contemplation reputed to bring answers to deep questions. It was two weeks after Terry died and my question as I walked and cried was, "Are you all right?" There was no answer. I tried to feel his presence again but nothing happened. Later, in our garden, it seemed that I could feel him around. But I wanted him to appear to me and reassure me that he was happy and even busy on the other side. It hasn't happened. A friend told me over lunch that maybe I hadn't seen him because we didn't have any unfinished business. I don't know if that is true, but I still wish he could have come around to let me know he's OK.

Take all the time you need and want for a generous goodbye.

Our goodbye would have to be an original, then, created not in the heat of the moment but over the course of time. I would have to let it build and find a life of its own. What would be forever lost are words I needed to hear from him. Imagining what he would have said is not quite the same, but over time I have come to accept that it is what it is, and that will have to do.

Honoring what we were seems to be the place to begin. We discovered each other over time and learned what mattered to us. It happened so slowly that in some ways I wasn't even aware of it until he was gone. We were strong individually and together. We were weak with bad habits and nasty behaviors that we recognized but hopefully corralled in the circle of our marriage. We were interesting to each other and respectful and forgiving. We held each other's hearts together when we lost our first baby and suffered alone when Terry was drafted during the Vietnam War. He gave me big chances to start over, and I cut him slack when he needed it. He jumped in as the primary parent when I went to graduate school. I was his best customer and strawberry seller at our farmers market. He became a Democrat for me, and I joined Rotary for him. It's not like we tried to convince each other to do things. It just happened. That's what I have to say goodbye to. It's nothing less than the structure and fabric of my life.

Making the goodbye real

On a plane heading east on Memorial Day of 2003, I wrote my first goodbye letter to Terry. Memorial Day and his birthday fell on the same weekend, so Tracey invited me to "get out of Dodge" and spend the weekend with her in New Jersey. It was my first trip alone after Terry died, and in that private/public space I wrote two pages of thoughts that I wished I could have shared with him.

We had been a team and had been married more than thirty-nine years. We'd been together so long and had gotten married so young that I didn't have a clue who I would be without him. Also, our marriage might have been made in heaven, but we certainly lived in the real world. We loved and respected each other, but we butted heads on all kinds of things. He was an oldest child and a leader of everything, and I was an only child who didn't especially like to be led. He had decided he wanted to do more boating, maybe for weeks at a time, and I wanted none of that. Boating was his passion. I, on the other hand, had a business to run. And even though our two cats are reputed to be descended from the original Viking mousers, I claimed they did not want to be boaters. Writing to him made the goodbye more real, and I read it over and over, adding and changing words, crying on it until the paper looked soaked by rain.

One of the most powerful ways to say goodbye happened when a good friend asked if I wanted her to come to the house and bless the place where Terry fell. It was such a gift to have her guide me in making a sacred place out of one that was so sad. We lit candles and focused on the joy of his life rather than the sadness of his leaving. The irony of the place is that it is one of the most beautiful in our yard. Terry died surrounded by spectacular beauty. I almost couldn't stand that at first, but over time it has given me comfort.

Near the fireplace in the great center of our house, I keep a picture of Terry. For a year the urn holding his ashes sat beside the portrait. A vase of fresh flowers, sometimes from the yard and sometimes from the grocery store, also graces the spot. I've never gone there to talk with him, but it's a place of honor. For a long time I also kept the basket of sympathy cards in the same area. I liked having all of that love in one place. Having something tangible to look at felt like another way to say goodbye.

The big goodbye

On the weekend of July 4, 2003, we flew to Kauai with more than half of Terry's ashes. The funeral home had divided his ashes, to my great relief, but I still worried about getting through airport security with the copper urn in my carry-on bag. We had a letter from the funeral home stating what it was and giving me permission to cross state lines with cremains, but still I worried. When we sailed through, I burst into tears of relief. We were on our way to the big goodbye. On July 5, fourteen relatives and friends were ferried out to a small commercial boat just at sunset. It had been windy all week, but on that evening the water was smooth and the winds were calm. Terry loved a great martini, and his favorite vodka was Grey Goose, so I brought along a bottle. We went the rounds sharing our thoughts about him before I put his ashes and the last bit of vodka in the beautiful waters of Hanalei Bay. As we saw his ashes spread and sink, we covered them with leis we made with love that morning.

Five months later on a sunny, cold December day, Tracey, Brandon, and I trudged around our local cemetery looking for just the right place to put more of Terry's ashes closer to home. We rejected spot after spot for one reason after another until finally we announced, "This is it."

SURVIVAL TIP

Trust yourself as you discover how you would like to move forward.

It didn't look like anything remarkable, but it felt really good. It was in the sun, guarded by two fir trees, and the people around him were young. "He'd like this place," we all agreed.

As the first anniversary of his death approached, I felt the weight of the day in my heart and body. Time, that force that was supposed to be my ticket to peace, was standing still while my heart was gently guiding me. Terry's urn needed a final, permanent resting place near our home in the city he loved so much. My heart told me to gather together the kids and a few close friends to share one final message of love at the small concrete vault that would keep his ashes safe. In the cardboard box holding his urn we tucked love notes, goodbye letters, poems, two CDs from his memorial service, a picture of him, a stuffed duck, a purple velvet heart, and a small seashell. We gathered around the shiny, black granite marker that marked his grave and said our last goodbyes. Then we went home to eat and celebrate with a bottle of expensive champagne. We were amazed we could pour sixteen glasses of champagne out of that one special bottle. Terry

Take action.

always liked to make good things last.

A month later on Terry's sixty-third birthday we gathered one last time at what he called the home place, the farm in Oklahoma where he grew up. His last dream the morning he died was of that farm. The wheat fields and rolling plains shaped his spirit and his sense of community. Terry's dad told stories about his childhood—about how Terry once held control of a tractor even while yellow jackets pursued him, or how he ran away to visit his grandma when he was barely three. We cried together and our tears fell on the same pasture grass as his ashes. Part of us would always be with part of him.

SURVIVAL TIP

Include other people.

Terry would have loved being in so many places, and for the rest of us, this last trip home brought more closure. It was a journey of celebration, grieving, sadness, loss, and discovery of who he was to us and who we are now as we move on with our own lives. Tracey saved a few of his ashes, for herself and for me, but I gently declined. For me it was time to let him go. I was done, and it felt right to admit that silently to myself and out loud to the kids.

So the goodbyes took on some texture and color over time, making the rainbow that I wanted. They were words spoken out loud, alone, and to people who loved Terry. They were in original writing and with the help of Hallmark. They were sung by such artists as Van Morrison, Billy Joel, and Willie Nelson. They were done with flowers and with balloons. They were eaten and toasted. They sat on the fireplace hearth and were in the form of pictures. They were felt and acted out. They were done from Hawaii to New York City, from Germany to Australia, and everywhere they showed tenderness and love. The celebration felt complete, and I achieved the goodbye I wanted. You'll know when your goodbyes are done, as well.

Questions to ask yourself as you say goodbye:

1. What was left unsaid by you? By the person who left?

2. What can you do to help the goodbye feel real?

3. Who will help you?

4. Where do the goodbye rituals need to take place?

5. What has helped you say goodbye in the past?

Step Three: Choose to Live

"It's not fair. You got to go first! We agreed that because you are a better cook and have all these businesses to manage that I would get to go first! How could you have gone back on our deal? It's not fair," I yelled at him over and over again in my head. "Do you get it that I didn't sign on to be left behind?" What I wanted most was to trade places with him. I felt like life had cheated me because he went first and I had to be left behind. Of course, none of this is rational. I have so many reasons to live, but in the early days, the pain was so intense that I just wanted to get away from it. Life wasn't fair, and I was angry at the hand I had been dealt.

I remember lying in bed one night thinking that sooner or later I would probably choose life. I didn't feel ready to make any grand pronouncements, but I decided at that moment to say out loud, "OK, I choose to live." No shooting stars greeted my statement, and the earth didn't shake, but there was a tiny shift inside of me. I made the choice to keep breathing and accepted that life wasn't done with me quite yet. Choosing to live obviously meant more than just breathing. It meant choosing to be really alive, and I didn't have a clue what that meant for me without Terry. I knew how to be his wife, how to play on his team, how to support and love him, how to enjoy his love, but I didn't know what life would look like without him. Even though I own and run my own business, have my own identity in the community, and have enough birthdays behind me to supposedly have wisdom, I had no idea how to be just me. Frankly, I was too scared to even think about it. So, I didn't. I read romance novels and drank too much Shiraz.

Make a written
inventory of the
things that are
good in your life.

It took months for the muddy waters to start to clear. I'm a strong believer in a natural order, so as the days grew longer, so did my time to think, to expand the definition of who I am, and to take the risk of letting in the answers.

When I look back even on the early days, I see evidence of my strength and character peeking through the pain. Just after Brandon left, I made my first journey into the yard. By the steps leading down to our garden, Terry had transplanted a huge plant of pampas grass that reached over the garden path and scratched my arms on every trip. I never liked that plant and had asked Terry a half-dozen times if he would move it. He always had some reason to put it off. That day I spied the pampas grass and hiked back up the hill to grab a shovel. I finally freed the root ball some two hours later but couldn't tip it into our rickety old wheelbarrow. So I grabbed two handfuls of its sharp spikes and dragged them across our property to the weed pile. Then I puffed back to the hole and carefully smoothed over the dirt. Looking back, it was a first step, even though I didn't know it at the time. I was doing things *my* way.

Focus on
your positive
qualities. It will
give you energy
to know that you
are your own
good friend.

Next up: the house we shared. Remember, when Terry died our bedroom was torn apart, waiting to be turned into a romantic hideaway. We had ordered carpet and stone for around the new fireplace. We already had a tile floor in the adjoining bathroom the length of the bathtub. Terry loved the tile because his good friend installed it, but I didn't like the fact that it was cold on my feet at night. "Well, guess what, Ruthann? Even though you didn't ask for it, it's your house now," I muttered to myself. So when it was time to install the carpet, I asked the contractor about removing the tile and extending the carpet to include the area in front of the tub. He told me that his installers could do it, but at $49 an hour. I looked at that tile and made a beeline for my toolbox. In it I found a chisel

Start to pay attention to those talents and personality traits that are uniquely yours. Hint: The parts of us that are as easy as breathing are our natural traits. Sometimes because they are so easy for us, we think they are equally easy for everyone. Not true. They're easy because they are our gifts.

Look for small things you can do that reflect what is important to you.

and a hammer.

Three days later, I had a big box of loose tiles and a floor ready for carpet. Every night since, I'm grateful for my early willingness to listen to and honor what I wanted.

That willingness also helped solve a mystery. Have you ever looked for the answer to a question and suddenly the right thing to do pops into your mind? A bright answer to a puzzling dilemma came to me one night at about 10 p.m.

We had a seventy-seven-inch-wide bedroom dresser with no place to live and a closet with inadequate storage. We had signed up California Closet Company to help solve the problem, but that appointment on the day Terry died didn't happen. For days I roamed the house looking for a place to put the dresser. I even considered putting it in the living room. On the night I stood staring into our closet, the answer became absolutely clear: Put it in the closet. I first took out the drawers and then let gravity help drive it down a half flight of stairs from Tracey's room. Then I maneuvered it around three corners and wiggled it into the tight closet space. Oops—a quarter inch too wide. Now what? There had to be a way to make it fit, and there was. With the help of three little wood blocks and a bit of perspiration, I managed to make it fit.

Be open to inspiration and those ideas that just come to you.

Now every time I look at it, I see a problem solved and give thanks for gravity. How did I think that dresser might fit in the closet? I have no idea, but I kept asking the questions, and somehow the answers kept coming.

Questions to ask yourself as you decide to live:

1. What do I have in my life that might make it worth living?

2. When I made a decision in the past that worked out well for me, how did I do it? What steps did I take? Can I follow a similar plan that will help me make this most important decision?

3. What is one thing about me that is unique?

4. What am I willing to try?

5. What needs to be done to make my world reflect who I am?

Step Four: Let Love In

All the love and all the sadness, fear, and aching loss came at me together, as though I were riding through space feeling the sun while looking deep into space all at once. While it was overwhelming, I felt so grateful. The loss was fact. The love was a gift. I had to figure out how to let it in, to receive it and let it do its healing work.
Brandon stayed as long as he could but eventually had to fly back to L.A. The next chapter of my life was waiting to begin. By then the crowd of loved ones was gone and what Terry often called "the gathering place" was big and empty. On a good day, a trip to the airport would take about forty-five minutes each way. After I took Brandon there to catch his plane, I wanted the traffic to be so bad it would take me weeks to get home. About halfway home the significance of this journey hit me, and I started to cry. Don't ask me how, but I made it to our driveway and into the garage. I got up enough nerve to get out of the car and consciously put one foot in front of the other, until they moved me the twelve feet to the back door.

SURVIVAL TIP

Let your body move—to music, with friends, with a dog, from further out in the parking lot.

Once inside, it wasn't quite as bad as I had feared. Fear does powerful things to the heart and mind. It makes the shadows bigger and the night darker than it really is. I had to remember that quiet has always been my friend, and this was the first time I had any quiet to myself since Terry died. This quiet felt big and deep and different, but I hoped it would be friendly, because I felt really alone.

There wasn't any place to go other than into my life as it was at that moment, even if that meant facing the empty house and the new life that was nothing but questions.

SURVIVAL TIP

Look for love in unexpected places.

That night, I climbed into bed and propped myself up on one pillow while I hugged another. It was the beginning of my life without Terry. Beside the bed was a basket of cards that had been pouring in from family and friends.

It was like Christmas, with one or two cards coming every day until the basket overflowed. I pulled the first card out of the basket and marveled at the love it contained. I pulled out another and another until cards blanketed the bed. Then I went the other way, re-reading each card and putting it back in the basket. The love in them washed over me, pouring some life back into the empty place in my soul. That love was strong and so real. It folded around me and kept me warm that first quiet night.

But what would other nights bring? I kept hoping Terry would come to me in a dream and tell me he was fine, even busy and in a beautiful place, but my nights never delivered that kind of visit. What they did was soften the thin web of control I had on my thoughts and questions. I'd think I was asleep only to jolt upright, seeing him falling, reaching for the gutter, feeling it slip out of his hands. What were his last thoughts? Did he have time to be afraid? Why didn't he jump clear of the ladder? I suspected his feet got tangled in the rungs. "Oh, my God, he's hitting the concrete with the back of his head. Oh, my God," I thought over and over and over. In my mind, he fell a thousand times, each time hurting all over again. Finally, I had the good sense to schedule an appointment with my family doctor.

SURVIVAL TIP

Find a good doctor.

He gently asked me how Terry died, and when I told him, he counseled me that Terry fell only once, was only hurt once. I let his words and the understanding behind them wash over me. Now, when I wake up in the night seeing Terry fall, I remember that it only happened once. Thank you, my dear doctor, for saying just the right thing at exactly the right time.

Love comes in many forms, and one of the gentlest came at night, when my two cats stretched full-length beside me, one on each side as I tried to sleep.

Consider adopting a pet. It will save them and you, too.

They put up with my tossing and turning and emitted sweet, loud, rumbling purrs whenever I woke them. Their purring told me I wasn't really alone, that something alive loved me. Every night, it comforted my heart.

Love is everything. One of the questions that kept surging out of my core was, "With no husband, who will love me?" I'd heard stories about friends melting away. Would that happen to me? Was I lovable enough on my own? I know how to be a wife and part of a couple, but can I find a way to be appealing as a friend or a lover again? The other question I never expected was, "Who will I love?" In my gathering place, who will I include? These questions demanded time. I had lots of that during long evenings and longer weekends. But I didn't always want to think. I wanted to escape, so I read a boatload of romance novels and decided Nora Roberts was my new favorite author. She gave me hope and kept me company.

So did my friends. In those early days a friend called, asking, "What can I do?" I answered, "You can get me some waterproof mascara." "Are you sure?" she asked. "Yes," I snapped. "You asked what you could do and that's it." Where did those words come from, that tone of voice? Would that kind of response drive people away? I didn't mean to be rude, but I just didn't have the energy to negotiate. It was an early act of trust that I could be honest with the people around me, and that they could cut me some slack if the words didn't come out right. It's such a gift to let people be raw without asking them to put a pretty face on every conversation.

One afternoon my office phone's "beep, beep, beep" announced, "You've got voice mail." Good friends called to say that they had been married twenty-three hours and fifteen minutes.

If you have the opportunity to celebrate someone or remember them with a card, do it. It will mean the world to them and will give you a lift, too.

They were on a road trip on their way to a convention, and the route took them close to Reno. They spotted a place called Chapel of the Bells and decided to get married. "Oh my gosh, did she really say Chapel of the Bells?" I wondered aloud. I had to listen to the message twice. Then I dropped everything and drove the mile to our bank to look at our marriage license in the safety-deposit box. There it was in the upper left corner: "Chapel of the Bells, November 29, 1963." These dear friends ended up marrying at the same place where Terry and I had wed forty years earlier! What are the odds of that happening without a little help from above? I'm thinking Terry whispered, "Turn in here," and they did. I hope they make it forty years. Letting myself be happy for them was evidence that their love added brightness to my days, as well. It felt so good to celebrate with them and to be lifted into their happy place for a while.

Might food also let love in? If you had given me a choice in the early days after losing Terry, I would happily have lived on chocolate-chip cookie dough straight from the package.

Eat something good for you every day.

Peanut butter on a spoon worked well, too. The idea of cooking real food appealed to me, but the thought of eating alone didn't, even on the one evening I tried candles and wine. I ended up losing thirteen pounds, and my body liked being thinner, but it took time to figure out this food thing. For a long time, actual meals mostly consisted of cooked spinach with cream cheese or breakfast cereal. Sometimes I'd cook a huge pot of soup and eat it for every meal that week. I also fixed hamhocks and beans. I figured there wasn't anyone to care if I ate beans. One sign that life was coming back into balance came after

Brandon advised me to get a small George Foreman grill and showed me how to cook chicken on it. Between the grill and good stuff to cook from our local farmers market, I got back into eating real food. Eating well truly was another way to bring in some love.

Friends and counselors who specialize in grief work told me six months would be a low point. It wasn't, though I sometimes thought it was, because I had cried every day and embarrassed myself by falling apart in public a half dozen times. Also, several things conspired to give me comfort and a false sense of emotional well-being, including my sixtieth birthday party. Terry had been talking about a party for me before he died, so friends and family came from far and near to help me celebrate. I felt so loved and it lofted me over the pain for weeks. On top of the party, Brandon gave me an unusual birthday gift.

I've always been curious about spiritual things, so maybe that is why I loved the fact that his gift was a psychic reading. He knew about a psychic from his friends in the movie industry and thought I would find her insight entertaining, possibly interesting, and maybe even inspiring. Because she lives in Georgia and I live in the Northwest, we met by telephone at sunset on October 16, exactly six months after Terry died. I fully expected the reading to revolve around Terry. But, no. About twenty minutes into the one-hour session, she told me Terry had picked out a new man for me. From that point on most of her guidance was about the new man. She gave me everything but his name and address. On the one hand, it felt like hope spelled in neon and capital letters. On the other hand, it drove my grieving into the background. I was thrown into the future before I was ready. Though her prediction had all the promise of spring, my heart knew I wasn't done missing Terry. Still, her gift gave me another breather in a sad time, and for that I will always be grateful.

Questions to ask yourself as you let love in:

1. What are three things I can do to take loving care of myself?

2. When people reach out to me, what is my natural reaction? Accept or reject?

3. What time of day do I need love the most?

4. What are healthy diversions for me (reading, exercise, hobbies, pets)?

5. Who are the professionals I can go to for support?

Step Five: Learn to Answer the Question, "How *Are* You?"

The first time someone asked me "How are you?" after Terry died, I just looked at her. I really didn't know how to answer. Not believing in stock answers and because the simple answer wasn't "Fine," I found myself wondering what to say. It happened over and over. Sometimes my answer was, "It's like taking in night and day all at once," because all the sadness, pain, heartache, and confusion accompanied acts of generosity, kindness, love, and friendship. Letting it all in was at best rich and at worst overwhelming. When my life was the bleakest, the people around me were absolutely at their best. To be sure, their kindness was the spark for my self-discovery.

Later, I found that people were still generous in wanting to reach out and ask how I was doing. But their question and concerned expression still put me in a bind. If it was a good day, and I did have a few, I felt somehow disrespectful admitting it. If it was a bad day, and there were some lulus, even a little bit of sympathy or a hug would leave me in a weeping heap.

SURVIVAL TIP

If you fall apart when someone asks how you are, give yourself a hug and forget it.

How I hated to fall apart in public. Even so, I remember the horrified expression on someone's face when I once answered, "I feel like all of my skin has fallen off and is lying shredded at my feet. I am raw and don't have a clue when new skin will grow or how it will look." Imagine the look I got. In hindsight, a different answer might have been easier on the person who asked.

Sometimes I would just say, "Fine," because that was all I was willing to share. It worked well on those occasions when I just wanted to point the conversation in a neutral direction, or when someone was

Don't be afraid to answer, "Fine."

asking just to be polite. I found myself looking for clues in people's eyes to determine how to answer.

About five months after Terry died, I started seeing an experienced grief counselor. Being a counselor/coach myself, I'm a believer in "paid friends," and I'll never forget her assessment of my situation during our first session. She described me as a "high-functioning griever." I have no reason to doubt her, but if that is true, my heart aches for people who are not. The words "high functioning" implied I was doing well when, the truth was, every morning I had to decide again to get up, get dressed, feed the cats, eat breakfast, and go to work. Maybe it's the routine that put me at the office door each morning. It sure didn't stop the tears. I cried every day for six months. Sometimes the tears came in a trickle, but mostly they came in a flood. Music often poured out a fresh batch: Billy Joel's "Lullaby," Willie Nelson and Merle Haggard's song "Pancho and Lefty," anything by Van Morrison.

Decide which music you most want to hear. For some it will be anything that reminds you of who you lost because it brings him or her closer. For others, it will be anything but that.

Terry loved all those singers and I would just lose it listening to them. Around the six-month mark, the Eagles came out with "Hole in the World." Well, there sure was a hole in my world, and I cried every time I heard the song. When I asked my counselor how to answer the "How-are-you?" question, she advised me to say, "As well as can be expected." It seems like a good response, and though it never really resonated with me, it is probably just the right answer for someone else, so I pass it on.

I do think "How are you?" is a different question when asked away from home.

Among strangers it usually means, "Who are you?" How can I answer that question and not talk about losing

Take a short trip. I call it "Getting out of Dodge."

Terry? How much do strangers really want to know, and how much do I want to endure their sad, compassionate, or horrified looks? There are no solid rules, so again I watch for clues and trust I will take my part of the conversation in the most positive direction. I do know it's easier to leave home and this life once in awhile if I'm going to be with my kids. My time with them is filled with different routines, with eating out or doing unusual things. On one trip, my grandson, Ben, looked me in the eye and called me "grandma" for the first time.

SURVIVAL TIP

Find a kid to laugh with.

He also tried being silly, chortling that both his mom and I had poopy pants. I didn't know an eighteen-month-old could already have a sense of humor, but Tracey, Ben, and I just laughed and laughed. A month or so later, Ben told his dad, "I'm funny." And he's right.

"How are you?" is a question I also ask myself on occasion. On a recent flight I felt tired, cranky, and sore. The three flight attendants talked so loudly that I couldn't sleep. I couldn't find peace with the music from the earphones, and I wondered if they knew how annoying they were to those of us trapped within earshot. Then I wondered what *I* do that is equally annoying. Some of the answers are obvious and some are hard. But as I used the airplane time to think and write honestly about how to make my life better, the loud voices behind me lost their power to annoy and blended in with the rest of the airplane noises.

I found out more about making life better when I returned to work after three weeks. I've heard of companies that only give their employees four days off after the loss of a loved one. I frankly don't know how those people can even function. At work there were daily opportunities to answer the "How-are-you?" question, and mostly I kept my answer honest but short. The clients were there to get help with their pain, so again I found the right answer depends on who is asking. On several occasions my clients didn't know about Terry, and I didn't tell them. One client had even fallen off his own roof, and I really wanted to share my story and ask more about that time in his life, but that wasn't why he was there, so I held back. I found a core strength beginning to come through and evidence that I could put my own grief aside to care for others. I was comforted to know I was bigger than my loss, and that someday, I guessed, the loss would be just a part of me. For the longest time, though, it seemed like loss loomed larger than any other part.

Another reason the "How-are-you?" question is so difficult is that the answer changes, season by season, day by day, sometimes minute by minute. One day almost a year after Terry died I wrote in my journal: "I am finally slowing down enough to find out how I am today. Some days alone in the house with the cats and the silence I wonder if my feet will ever find a new path to explore. So, I slow down but it doesn't give me much comfort. I've always been a doer and with Terry there were always more ideas ready to cook than burners to cook them. But that was then. Now I'm wondering if my own well of ideas will ever produce again. It's terrifying to sit and sit. It's also boring. I've been willing to endure being stalled because it's been winter and our Northwest days only last eight hours. But the days are starting to grow longer and I'm afraid to face a sixteen-hour day. I've also endured the boredom because creating my own life scares the hell out of me. It's just so big! So I sit here waiting for the bell to ring, the light to turn green, waiting for life to find me and for me to find out who I am."

Even now, I am still playing with my answer to "How *are* you?" I usually start with "Thank you for asking. Every day is different, and today I am. . ." and then pick the most appropriate phrase:
> doing OK;
> having a hard time;
> doing fine; or
> up and down.

Sometimes I even say, "Do you really want to know?"
I follow it up with, "And how are *you*?" That's my latest version. As

you go along, trust that you will find the words that will work for you. If you want to use my words, consider them yours.

Questions to answer as you figure out how to answer "How *are* you?":

1. What are three ways that you might answer this question, depending on who is asking, where you are, and what you want to reveal?

2. Are you more visual or more auditory? In other words, is it easier for you to pick up clues from someone else's expression or from what they say? Your answer will help you know the best way to pick up clues about where another person is coming from.

3. How are you going to check in with yourself? Do you ask yourself questions or trust your body to let you know what is going on with you at any given time?

4. What are you doing to give yourself a break once in a while?

5. How do you respond to the changing seasons? How do the seasons influence how you are?

Step Six: Accept the Truth

"Who am I if I'm not married?" An incident shortly after my sixtieth birthday gave me a chance to see myself in action and find out more about who I am and what this world of widowhood might be like. I own the building that houses my office, and one Monday I arrived to find that one of my tenants had unexpectedly moved out during the night. By day's end, all I wanted was to get home and take a hot bath. But I had another life lesson in store.

The left front tire of my car was flat. After getting no help and some bad advice from a guy at a nearby auto-parts store, I considered calling AAA, but I just wasn't in the mood to wait. So, I moved the car away from the front door of the shop and gamely opened the trunk. In my two-inch heels and a dress, I got out the tools and went to work. After all, I proudly put on my own snow tires for ten years. I remembered: Loosen the lug nuts first before jacking up the car. As usual, the lug nuts were on so tight I had to put the lug wrench on each one and stand or even jump on the tool until the nut loosened. I was well on my way to finishing when a man came along. He asked what I was doing, which seemed pretty obvious, so I just looked at him.

SURVIVAL TIP

Give people enough time to be helpful. And remember: Laugh at the dumb stuff they do, because some of it will be unbelievable.

"Well, where's your husband?" At this point, he was on thin ice. "He died six months ago," I practically shouted. "Oh," he said, not skipping a beat. Then he asked, "Do you go to church? You need Jesus Christ as your Lord and Savior." I shot back that I simply needed a tire that would hold air, but the personal questions kept coming. With sweat now running down my face, my hands black and grimy from the dirty tires, and my back aching, he had the gall to ask my age, so I told him.

"Well, my daughter is fifty-eight and I can't imagine her changing a tire. My hat is off to you!" He ambled off and I just stared after him. Pretty soon I was on my way, but I learned a thing or two that day. The truth is that I'm not afraid to tackle a challenge. I have experience that I can draw on. I can think of alternative solutions if my first idea doesn't work. And if I give people a chance, many of them will make this journey a whole lot more interesting, knuckleheads notwithstanding.

The toughest part of digging for truth is that so much of it is hard to find. So I ask myself questions and then wait. Real answers take their own sweet time. And I hate that. I want to know right now that everything is going to be fine. Even more, I want to know what "fine" will mean down the road. Anything could be around the next corner, and in the middle of the night I always imagine it is something big, hairy, and scary. I could end up a bag lady pushing what's left of my earthly belongings in a shopping cart I stole from the grocery store, or I could find a wonderful man who wants to share his life with me. All of these questions can be filtered through fear or hope. God, let me choose hope.

I especially needed hope on my first Thanksgiving without Terry, because two days later would have been our fortieth anniversary. Terry and I planned to be in New Jersey with Tracey, Steve, and Ben, and then go into New York City for a Broadway play and a fancy dinner. I went ahead with those plans, inviting the family to join me. Dinner was first. What did I eat? I don't have a clue. How was the play? Terrible. Plus, the bottom was about to drop out of my life, and I didn't see it coming. Was I letting in the truth? Not even close. The next day I was packing to fly home when I looked down at my wedding ring. I always loved it. It was a relic of my youth, cast using the "lost wax" technique with small tumbled garnets held firmly in gold swirls. Looking at the ring, I whispered to myself, "Face it, Ruthann, you're no longer married. Take it off." So, I gently slid the ring off my finger and placed it in my cosmetic bag.

Do the hard things that come from accepting the truth. It's so much easier to have them behind you.

I usually get my suitcase through security and into the overhead bins on a plane with ease, but this time I found myself wanting to use only my right hand and hide my ringless left hand in my pocket. On the plane I felt unprotected and hardly said a word the whole trip. In the parking lot, ready to drive home, I bent over the steering wheel and sobbed, not wanting to go home to that empty house and my empty life. But I did. For weeks after, I felt for that phantom ring, but finally my hands and heart accepted that our rings belonged together, in a small, silk pouch tucked away in a safe place.

My feeling of loss only seemed to deepen. As winter dragged on, I hid away in the house, and I almost got away with it. I'd go to work, then come home and crawl into bed at 6:30 p.m. Sometimes I slept so long that my back hurt. I let voice mail take calls. I ate peanut butter out of the jar for dinner and washed it down with wine.

Be honest with your friends.

Fortunately, I had one good habit and one good friend. I walked two mornings a week with a woman who is both a counselor and a psychiatric nurse. On one of our walks, she asked how I was doing, and fortunately I was honest with her. She said I sounded depressed and asked if I would consider antidepressants. I followed her advice and believe today that she saved my life. Within days, I started to breathe again, to eat, to stop drinking, and to rise above a world colored only in gray and filtered through sad sounds. The truth was, I was depressed and needed help. Still, Christmas was coming in two weeks, and my mom, the kids, and their families were all flying in. By December 21, all I had done was buy a wreath on sale. Brandon and my mom arrived at the airport an hour apart, and on the way to the car I admitted to Brandon that Christmas was nowhere near arriving at our house. He stared at me, then took charge. By the time the rest of the family arrived two days

Be tender and listen to what is right for you.

later, we had a decorated tree and house, wrapped presents under the tree, more than enough food, and Christmas music on the stereo. My mom and Brandon were stars, and I was along for the ride. We decided to honor Terry with special ornaments on the tree and toasts at every meal. Someone even suggested that we leave his place empty at the table. But I just couldn't do that. He was gone, but to see it that way was just too hard.

Get some poster board, glue, and a stack of magazines, and ask, "Where does my life want to take me from here?" Then, put on some good music, light a candle, and make yourself a collage. Know that you can still join my choir if you choose to ignore this suggestion, but I think you'll be pleased with the results.

Our lives would always have an empty place where he should have been. We were feeling our way as a family, and you will, too.

Right-brain wisdom
Sometimes, when I'm with creative clients I ask them to put together a collage of pictures. All it takes is poster board, glue, and magazine pictures that touch their hearts. The hard part is finding the willingness to work on a project that feels a bit flaky. But I recommend it to give the creative, intuitive part of the mind a voice. Our culture is so left-brained that this gentle, creative voice from our right brain is often discounted and ignored. Yet, the messages from this part of us can be mind-blowers. They are so positive and gentle that I am convinced they come from a reservoir of deep self-love.
In all the months I was hurting and trying to come to some truths, I had ignored the simple suggestion I had seen help so many clients. So one evening I lit candles, put some classical oboe music on my stereo, spread out all of the clippings from

Reward your effort. Every time you make an effort, do something nice for yourself. The idea is to keep putting energy back into your system so you will live and not just exist.

magazines on the carpet in my home office, and got started.

I wanted to honor my roots, celebrate Terry's place in my life, and see where my life wanted to go from here. The finished product astounded me. It was all bright colors and phrases about strength, hope, curiosity, and beauty. It's still a comfort to look at, and I have spent a lot of time pondering its message to me. Sometimes its message of hope seems to be for some *other* Ruthann, but mostly I am eager to find out if it's true. I am still alive, and the challenge is to live the most authentic version of me I can discover.

My collage is a daily reminder to keep moving forward and pursue truth, even if it hurts. The risk is worth it. A big question remained for me, though: Was Terry ready to go? Some people had asked me if he might have known on some level that his life would soon end. He always talked about living to be 105, but I think he must have known something. A month before he died, he went to L.A. to help Brandon get out from under a car contract that trapped him in a terrible but high-paying job. Terry then drove Brandon's car to our home, stopping on the way to see cousins he hadn't seen for awhile. He made it home just in time to straighten out a business deal that had gone bad. He and I had visited Tracey, Steve, and Ben just eight days before he died. He let Dixie talk him into a better life insurance policy—without it I'd be doing something much different than writing this book. He finished the taxes earlier than usual, and we had wild, wonderful sex the night before he died. In short, he'd cleared up a lot of loose ends. So, was he ready to go? For the time he had, he lived with intensity, purpose, and generosity. I hope people will be able to say the same about me when I go. Is that a guiding truth? Possibly.

Questions to ask yourself as you accept the truth:

1. How will I know the truth when I see/hear/think it?

2. How am I going to take care of myself during this challenging time?

3. What are my personal resources and good habits that will help?

4. What will be hard and how do I want to manage?

5. Where will I find the patience to hang on until life gets better?

Step Seven: Want More!

Terry hadn't been dead a month when someone remarked to me, "You two had such a good marriage. You've had the good life once. I can't imagine it being possible twice." At the time I just nodded. What else is there to do with someone who is trying to steal hope? There is no real way to refute that kind of statement except to know I want my life to go on. I want more—more love, more opportunity to laugh and cry with someone who loves me, more time to explore our amazing world, and more time to give back. I also want more for Terry, perhaps by keeping his legacy alive.

Terry's "shop local" motto drove me crazy. It makes perfect economic sense, because our city is young and its tax base is small. But I like going across town to discount and gourmet-food stores. He was chairman of our city economic development commission and was excited about spreading his passion for shopping locally. When he died, his spot on the commission needed to be filled, and the city council asked me to fill it. It was a generous offer, and when I agreed, it felt like I was keeping Terry's legacy alive.

Terry also had a sense of humor, and when he and Dixie got together, anything could happen. The Duck Parade is a perfect example. Terry decided the farmers market needed more customers, and a parade would be the perfect way to make that happen. I have no idea where the notion came from, but in 1999 they decided to hold a parade the first Saturday in June, which they hoped would signal the end of our legendary rainy season. Now, years later, the Duck Parade draws people dressed in duck outfits, the high school band "ducking" their heads after they play each song, and floats on trucks featuring ducks. Anything yellow goes, and we love the garbage trucks as much as the dogs dressed like ducks. The duck has become our city mascot, and when the new city center is built, there will be a duck big enough for kids to climb on in some prominent place in memory of Terry. I want all of that and more.

I also want Ben to know his Grandpa T. Terry loved him even though their time together was short. He was excited about teaching Ben to sail and to love the Northwest. I want Ben to know that Grandpa T. was passionate about making the world a better place. I want him to know that Terry loved Tracey, his daughter and Ben's mom, with a love so deep it will last forever. I want Ben to know that it doesn't matter that he won't be able to remember the times Terry held him or fed him or played with him. I still want Terry to be more than an empty place at the table. Tracey and Steve are helping with that, and they told me one of Ben's favorite video characters is Bob the Builder. Because they don't have a video character named Terry the Builder, I guess Bob will have to do.

SURVIVAL TIP

Be open to the unlimited ways more can come into your life. Let yourself be surprised.

Just because I want more doesn't mean I always know how "more" will happen in my life. For instance, Tracey and Steve invited me to fly across country to Florida to spend some time with Steve's mom and dad, who are now part of my extended family. My own family is small, so their generosity in letting me be part of their wonderful Jewish clan is a real gift. I love the stories and the laughing, the new family members, and the hugs. *They* are more, and it's a wonderful surprise to be surrounded by their love. I feel grateful.

After that trip, I made good on a commitment to be a speaker at the Northwest Organ Donor Association's semi-annual, in-house training session. Because Terry died suddenly, there was no automatic support for me, such as hospice. That's where the association came in.

Because he was an organ donor, the association's social worker could help me. She held my heart in her gentle hands more than once. I remember that when I couldn't find Terry's business checkbook and was frantic with fear, she talked me back from the cliff and got me

Consider becoming an organ donor. If you have a chance to carry out that request for a family member, give the gift of life to others.

breathing again until I could think. And of course, I found it right where Terry had left it. So when she asked me to represent the families of donors, it was easy to agree. As I was preparing for the presentation, I became aware of the gift the association had given to Terry, to our family, and to me: letting Terry continue his legacy of generosity because he had checked the organ-donor box on his driver's license. It is a precious opportunity. Being surrounded by those who made the organ donation possible and being able to thank them for the gift will always be one of the highlights of my life. We later got a letter from the woman who received Terry's left kidney, and she relayed how wonderful it was to have her life back. Terry's essence joined with hers when she got his kidney, and I believe all that positive passion for life and for making the world better is now part of who she is. I want more people to know about the gift of organ donation. It gives me intense joy to know Terry is still alive and still making the world a better place through the lives of everyday people. I want everyone to be willing to donate their organs when they no longer need them, and I want families to be willing to honor that request.

Finally, I want more from myself and for myself. For a long time, I wanted a new car, but never could decide on a model. My 1980 Datsun 280 ZX was a good and faithful companion for twenty-four years, but she was starting to leave me stranded, and most importantly, Ben couldn't fit in the back seat. Getting my new two-door, six-speed, arrest-me-red 2004 Infiniti G35 coupe with manual transmission was a collective adventure.

"More" is really a state of mind and a matter of giving yourself permission to have a world that is bigger than it is right now.

I had so many wonderful friends who stepped in to help me. My oldest friend suggested that particular car. Other friends took me to a car show, where I got a feel for it by sitting in a dozen of them. Someone else called a local Infiniti dealer to pave the way, and then finally a saleswoman walked me through the purchase, cheering me on when I first climbed behind the wheel. Lastly, I suspect Terry orchestrated when the car would arrive.

When I ordered it in spring, my saleswoman said it would arrive in July, nowhere near the one-year anniversary of Terry's death. Then she called back to say that the car was going to arrive early, around the third week of April. I whispered to myself, "Please, God, don't let it come on April 15." Brandon arrived on April 14 to help us take the rest of Terry's ashes to the cemetery, and when we got home from the airport, there was a phone message from my saleswoman. The car would be ready to pick up the next day, on April 15. "I don't think I can do this, Brandon," I cried when I heard the message. His reply set me free. "Mom, Dad is doing this for you, to bring something wonderful into your life on this sad day. I'll go with you, and we'll pick it up together." So, on April 15, the saddest day of the year, a bright and beautiful new car joined our family, and she is definitely "more."

Sometimes giving means "more." My faithful Datsun started her own new life with Bill's son in Hawaii. He's a mechanic and had always loved my car. Bill happened to be in town for a conference, so he helped me get the car ready for shipping and get her to the port after I took her to say goodbye to her mechanic and changed the license plate. Three weeks later, Bill and his son called to say they were driving her to her new home, and she was in perfect shape. So I called the shippers to thank them for a job well done. There was dead silence on the other end. "Oh my God, you are the first person who has ever called with good news," the man on the phone said. "Which car was it?" he asked. When I told him, he answered, "I remember that car!" Maybe

> **SURVIVAL TIP**
>
> Look for ways you can reach out and make someone's day. It's amazing how acts of kindness come back to make our days brighter, too.

more is as simple as giving a compliment. One thing is certain: It feels great.

Several months later, I signed up for a high-speed driving class in my hot new car, not only to see what she could do but to learn some advanced skills. My biggest fear was that I would embarrass myself. Because I was the only woman and the oldest student by at least thirty years, there was a chance I could have been a real dud. But I had challenged myself to take a risk and push myself to see how far and how fast I could go. It was amazing. Even though I tended to forget which gear I wanted to go into in the heat of the moment, I took her to ninety-five miles per hour and fell in love with her brakes. I only killed a cone once and broke another's arm a second time. After that, the cones were safe. I even navigated the dreaded second curve with its 45-degree angles without messing up and proudly received my certificate of graduation at the end of the day. I want more experiences to feel pushed to my limits and to test myself. I want to call on my courage and to risk learning new things:

To believe there is wisdom to the timing

To see around the bend in this river

To know I have a limited tolerance for intense anticipation

To trust I will stay the course

To use all my courage to sit still and let this time unfold at its own pace

To hope the future will be bright and generous

To ask life to give me a chance to be more, do more, live more

To promise I'll live with passion and love and goodness

To want to rush and know thankfully that I won't

Questions to ask yourself as you want more:

1. List what you want more of in your life. Put the easier things first.

2. How will you know when you have more?

3. What could stop you from having more?

4. What do you have to let go of to let in more?

5. Who do you want to spend more time with? When? How? Where?

Step Eight: Let Yourself Laugh

"I'm funny," Ben says about himself. And he's right. He crinkles his nose when he flashes one of his big smiles. He laughs with all the enthusiasm of a happy two-year-old. And the world is magic because he is in it.

SURVIVAL TIP

Find a child who will give you rainbow pictures, take you on a playground slide, and belly laugh until you have to join in.

Sometimes his sunshine reminds me of what Terry is missing, and the tears catch in my throat. I want to smile, but the sadness in that moment is bigger. I know it will pass, because life is teaching me that the color of laughter is brighter than the gray of tears. You'll find laughter will color your days, too, in the most surprising ways and at the most unexpected times.

Sometimes it arrives on cats' paws, such as those belonging to Humphrey Bogart and Katharine Hepburn. Bogey weighed in close to twenty-three pounds in his black-and-white tuxedo, and his sister, Katey, tipped the scales around twelve pounds. She had dainty white paws and freckles on her nose. During one of my lonely evenings, while they pinned me between them on our bed, I stroked Bogey's soft fur and made the mistake of saying, "Well, Bogey, I guess you're the man of the house now." Apparently he took me literally, because he started spraying random objects around the house: my robe in the closet, my shoes by the back door, the wall in the kitchen, the window by the front door. Then Katey would come along and roll in it, as though it were catnip or something. What a mess. I caught Bogey as he sauntered down the hallway one day, looked him in the eye, and said sternly, "You're no longer the man of the house. We're a team. No more spraying!"

It took a few days to sink into his kitty brain, but he finally stopped. Last time I'll tell a cat to take control.

You might say I also had control issues with Terry's old farm truck. It started out pink, so he got a good deal on it, but it was hardly a friend to the ladies. Even after he painted it green, it was neither beautiful nor dependable. But it did what he needed it to do for the farmers market, and now it was mine.

I misread its gauges, let it nearly run out of gas, griped when it died at stop signs, and wondered what the gremlin who lived under its hood was called. One winter day that truck and I got into a tussle. At the time, it sat on wet weeds in a lower meadow of our property and was filled with green logs. "You'll never make it up the hill," a neighbor said as I climbed behind the wheel to haul the wood closer to the house. "Just watch," I replied. I slipped the beast into second gear, aimed it uphill, and jammed my foot down on the gas pedal. We hit a couple of slippery spots, spun in the gravel, and bounced over the ruts in the muddy road, but the weight of the wood gave us the advantage we needed to reach solid ground. I can only imagine how it looked to bystanders, but it made my day. That one was worth a hoot of joy and a smile of gratitude.

Indeed, I am finding that I'm my own best source of laughter. I know I can be gullible, but usually things work out just fine. When a refrigerated pickup truck pulled into my driveway, unfortunately I was home. The woman in the passenger seat never even glanced my way, and that should have been a clue. The driver hopped out and announced that he had a deal for me. He said my neighbors down the street had just bought $188 worth of beef from him, and he was willing to give me the same good deal. Well, he did say it was *Angus* beef, and it sure looked good. And it never hurts to have good quality

Don't buy meat from a guy in a pickup.

meat on hand. So I wrote him a check on the spot and piled the meat into my freezer.

Weeks later, the family came for Christmas, and I proudly hauled out my stash of "prime beef." The filet mignon was so tough, even my mom wouldn't eat it, preferring hunger instead. In short, I ended up with $188 worth of meat no better than hamburger. The family asked me for days what else I bought from that guy in the pickup truck, apparently so they could be forewarned. We all laughed, but I also learned a lesson about handing over money to strangers. And I remembered to laugh at myself.

In those dark days after Terry's death, I also recognized how much I turned to cleaning to work out stress. I'm known to be a cleaning queen, but on one occasion I outdid even myself. Part of finishing the house after Terry died involved getting some new lights in the hallway. An electrician installed them; they looked beautiful and I loved them. I left for a few days, and when I returned, I noticed a big gray spot in the middle of the hallway. It looked as though the cats had thrown up on the spot and the stain was still in the carpet. My motto is "out spot," so I decided to get cleaning, despite the fact that it was 9:30 p.m. For thirty minutes I scrubbed, wiped, and brushed the carpet. As heaven is my witness, I even poured straight bleach on that spot.

Be careful where you pour bleach.

Nothing worked. It was impermeable. Or was it? On a creative whim, I glanced up at the new light hanging overhead and gave the hanging bulb a swing. The spot moved! I was stunned. I had been trying to bleach a shadow. I'm sure my angels had to work overtime to keep the bleach from rotting the carpet while they howled with laughter at my foolishness. And, quite frankly, I couldn't blame them.

Questions to ask yourself as you find some laughter:

1. Who is funny? How can you make time to be with them?

2. When the unexpected happens, what are the funny parts?

3. What color is your smile? Your laugh?

4. In the middle of the saddest moments, who can help you see through the darkness to the light?

5. What have you done that is just so silly you have to laugh at yourself?

Step Nine: Face Forward and Take Back Your Power

Pick a direction. I've always liked north. I love the Northwest and the North Star. I'll never forget flying north in a small floatplane to celebrate Terry's fiftieth birthday when we looked up and saw we were flying under an eagle. It was magic. Somehow, just picking a direction gives strength to a moment.

SURVIVAL TIP

Go outside and face the four directions, asking which one feels most powerful for you at this time in your life. Face that way, breathing in the power.

I stand in a spot, face north, and look up my driveway. It forces me to face the future, beyond this place where I can hide and pretend nothing has changed. It means I have said out loud that I choose to look out, at least some of the time. How long it will take for this to become the new reality is another question, but the journey has begun.

$P = I + E$

Since 1984, I have counseled and coached clients who wanted to take control of their lives, and I've become aware of two key ingredients in personal power. One is information and the other is energy. Together they conveniently work into an acronym I call my PIE formula. Not only do the letters actually stand for something delicious, but they're easy to remember.

P (Personal Power) = I (Information) + E (Energy)
Information includes what you need to know about both yourself (inside) and the world (outside). Information like this needs to be true, so it may require hard thinking or research. But we need real information to make quality decisions. Energy is the fuel of life. We

51

Think of your energy like fuel in your personal gas tank, or your available credit limit on your charge card. Make a list of all the positive things you want to do with it.

Choose the way you want to get news that leaves you feeling the least stressed. Also pick the time of day when you are most able to handle taking in the news of the world. Then choose not to take in news in other ways for a while.

need to know both what gives us energy and what takes energy away. Clients are jubilant when they give themselves permission to plug the energy leaks.

What I've found is that personal power, or knowing that we are in control of our own lives, is in direct proportion to the quality and quantity of information we have and the amount of energy we need to take action. If we are short on power, one of those two things is missing. During intense grief, both of these key components are in short supply. No wonder it is a scary time.

What is so immobilizing about the early days of intense and unexpected loss is the absolute lack of preparation. That is especially true if the loss is sudden. One minute life is normal and the next minute there is no normal. One minute you know you have to navigate your way through life's challenges, but even if they are hard they are still familiar. The next minute, nothing is familiar. The smallest acts of life are both an effort and a cause for new thinking. My information search started when I found I was hungry for other people's stories. How did they make their way through this scary time? I went online to find stories like mine, stories of people who were thrown into loss with no time to prepare.

None of the stories fit exactly, but even bits of ideas were better than nothing. So at night I read what I could find and by day I cried my way through weekly sessions with a grief counselor.

I learned that grief has a life of its own. Even though we go through numerous cycles of change, big loss is unique. I've seen clients react to losing their jobs with the same kind of intensity that I felt losing Terry, especially if they were caught by surprise. It is just a shattering blow, stripping away everything that identifies us. I learned that I could expect to be blindsided by intense feelings, and there was very little I could do to stop them. My first trip to the store to shop for groceries lasted about ten minutes. I couldn't make it through such a familiar routine without Terry. The first time I went out to dinner with friends and the hostess asked how many were in our party, I automatically said "four." When it hit me that there were only three, I almost made myself sick sobbing. I was learning about my limits and how many places the old normal no longer existed. I was also learning from the brave stories of others what might be down the road for me. I was looking for hope that the pain wouldn't last forever, so I will tell you now: The pain won't last forever. It will transform you, but it won't hurt this bad forever.

Sometimes hurt lets you see things more clearly. About a year before Terry died, I changed doctors. My old doctor had a habit of yawning when I talked to him and scolding me when I asked questions. The net result was I felt discounted and found myself not talking to him. When I chose my new doctor, I made a pact with him and myself that I would be completely honest. It has made for some uncomfortable moments, such as the time I told him about all the supplements I take for my brain, or the time I asked him some personal questions about sex. But it has been liberating. He treats me with respect and also has the information he needs to be really effective in his recommendations.

Like the light in a Coleman lantern, the flame of energy that we call on every minute to live our lives needs to be protected from what might try to blow it out. My natural flow of energy was especially low for the first year after Terry died. Any threat to it, whether my own fear, scary news about how the world was going to hell, or someone's complaining, just reduced the flame more. So I learned from necessity to be sensitive to what I could handle and what I couldn't. It meant I had to be assertive on several occasions, and that took some people by surprise. If it hadn't felt like survival to me, I might have backpedaled. On the other hand, I've learned that being honest with myself and honest in the choices I make feels much more consistent with the person I really am. It's another way of facing forward, but it's not an easy one.

Sometimes I surprise myself with what gives me energy. After the shock of 9/11, the simple act of baking a birthday cake for Dixie got me emotionally back on my feet.

Somehow, contributing to celebrating her birth got me back in touch with the possibility that goodness might still exist in the world. After Terry died, it took me awhile to make my first birthday cake again, but when I did, it felt like a piece of *me* was being reborn. Also, early on I learned that I love to build wood fires in the fireplace. The act of doing it and experiencing it ignites my own energy flame. As soon as the weather cooled, I built a fire every night and let the warmth fill the room and the sad places in my heart.

Another way I faced forward was to find anchor words that served as beacons for me when the night got too dark. When my counselor asked what my anchor words might be, I didn't have a clue. She reminded me that anchors keep us safely tied to shore when the current is too

> **SURVIVAL TIP**
>
> Do something every day that actively gives you energy. Consider rewarding your effort. That means tie rewards to energy expended and not to results. If you decide to reward yourself with a non-fat latte for making a stressful phone call and you get the person's voice mail, go ahead and get the latte. It took effort to make the call even if you didn't get results. I know it feels like a stretch, but try it sometime.

Find or make a card with your anchor words and then frame it.

strong, or we want to rest for the night. "A life needs to have some anchors," she said, "to help keep us safe and remind us what is important to us." After some thought, I came up with two: "courage" and "trust." Over time, though, I decided to substitute "gratitude" for "trust," because "trust" seemed to have the potential to make me vulnerable.

And I love the idea of facing life with gratitude, with a thankful heart and with the awareness that there is good in the world. These two anchors give me permission to face forward without being adrift. They have become my companions on this new journey.

Questions to ask yourself as you face forward and take back your power:

1. What direction gives you hope and faces you forward?

2. What information do you need about you? About the world?

3. What do you need protection from because it takes energy away?

4. What gives you energy?

5. What are your anchor words?

Step Ten: Move Ahead With an Open Heart

Moving ahead sounds as easy as walking from the car to your back door. In reality, it is an ongoing act of courage, hope, vision, and expectation. Hopefully we take some of the steps with people courageous enough to walk with us. They can open our hearts and pour in love when we can't do it for ourselves. The most surprising part of this adventure is finding the places of identity, strength, courage, and comfort.

Engaging my hands came first as I moved furniture and took out the tile to make room for new carpet in the bathroom. Taking out the old tile was a small, big step. It was a declaration of being alive, of ownership, and of hope for the unknown future.

SURVIVAL TIP

Do something with results you can see.

Engaging my mind came second, in bits and pieces, starting on the surface and teaching me gently. I discovered romance novels, forgot TV, and fell in love with new music. I played a few songs over and over. Van Morrison's "Steal My Heart Away" had me sobbing in the car, but I listened to it until it finally became part of my bridge to a hopeful future.

SURVIVAL TIP

Trust yourself to know which people you can say "yes" to as they reach out to you.

Loving people with the capacity to love back became the brightest gift.

Some amazing souls held steady, offering everything from morning walks and professional advice to daily calls and monthly lunches. I hope they are getting points in heaven. Even as they reached out to comfort me I was aware they loved and missed Terry, too. Death messes with us all.

How can we measure the depth of friendship when it is pure, from the heart, and so right that there will never be a way to pay it back? How do some people know just what to do and aren't afraid to do it? One special friend wasn't afraid to go to lunch with me and listen to me sob over salad and too much coffee. And he did it over and over again, once a month without fail. Gradually, I could make it through lunch without crying. What a relief. I'll be forever grateful that he was the kind of friend willing to step into the pit with me. He wasn't afraid, and I learned from his example that I didn't need to be afraid, either. What a gift his love was, and again I can't imagine the journey without the comfort of his monthly visits.

Friends sometimes come out of nowhere. Flying to California didn't seem like it should be so lonely. But staying at my mom's empty house while her hip healed in a nursing facility brought back a flood of memories. Terry was everywhere. He was with me the last time I was there, and his shaving cream and hair gel were still in the bathroom. I walked through the house and started to sob. My lifeline ended up being the amazing owner of the company I hired to advise me in finding good home care for Mom. I called the owner's cell phone once saying I couldn't handle being alone in that house.

Her reply freed me: "You can. Just take all

> **SURVIVAL TIP**
>
> Be willing to reach out to people and be honest if the load is too heavy. If you're sleeping all the time, not sleeping enough, eating too little, hiding at home, or displaying any other symptoms of depression, let people know. You might want to talk with your doctor, counselor, minister, or priest. If they suggest antidepressants for awhile, don't be afrid to consider giving them a try.

the time you need to enjoy your mom. You don't need to solve any problems today. Cry and laugh with her. Just be with her." OK, that's how it's done, one step at a time. Laugh and cry because life is both smiles and tears.

My neighbor is a similar problem-solver. She knows how to do the practical things. She figured out how to turn on the sprinklers on my property and then turned me on to splitting wood with her gas-powered log-splitter. She fed me when I didn't know I was hungry and brought my newspaper and mail to my door for months. At every turn in my life at home, she was there to help make sense out of the everyday stuff that would have piled up and taken me under.

SURVIVAL TIP

If you aren't able to be everything you want for a friend right now, let yourself off the hook. At some time in the future, you'll be able to pay it forward.

At the same time, she was unbelievably forgiving when I wasn't able to be there for her. When she needed me, I was still running on low and I just wasn't much help. It was bad timing and one of those life's-not-fair episodes, which I finally accepted. I had to hand her off to other people in her life who could be the kind of friends she needed, but I promised myself to step up to the plate for someone else when I got the chance.

Every evening for the first six months after Terry died, Brandon called me. He held out that lifeline and took his own heart in his hands every time he called. How did he have the wisdom and courage to know just how much I needed the connection with him? When did he become the man he is? It was a gift delivered at the perfect time, and I'll be forever grateful. Tracey, Steve, and Ben gave me a different kind of comfort, the kind built on awareness of family and hope for the future. They continue to help us build a new family unit, one that honors Terry but looks forward without him. They include me in the family they are building, and I feel lucky.

I eventually started telling people that I had turned a corner from aching all the time to being grateful for the time Terry and I had together. They were noble words that wanted to root around and seep into my heart, but sometimes they had trouble finding the way. So, one night when I couldn't sleep, I let the random memories that wanted to be treasured float up in my mind. I remembered the first time Terry put suntan lotion on my shoulders and the way his hands looked, finding him like a beacon in the crowd when I graduated from college, the look on his face when we threw him a surprise party, dancing in the gravel at the farmers market. The magic lasted an hour before sleep finally won, but I woke in the morning feeling grateful first, before I cried.

Sometimes I think angels weep to see us struggle so hard to put a face on this life, making our way through the endless days and nights. They must wonder at our lack of wonder and send rippling laughter out to the edge of light when we celebrate. I know now that life is magic, a space between, an impossible gift. It is arguably the easiest and the hardest thing we'll ever do. It's the easiest because all it takes is the simple act of breathing in, pausing, and breathing out. It's the hardest because the pause is filled to overflowing with expectations, thoughts, feelings, and desires. Moving through the islands of pauses eventually wears us out, and the ultimate pause is what happens without the breath. That's my sense, anyway. No one really knows, but I think life and its fullness can't be contained by just one experience.

Is there any truth to reincarnation? Someday it will be my turn to find out. The silence in the eyes of someone whose life is over says everything about the magic that life is. Who could ever see that spark leave and not know of its compelling gift? So, what I know is that we are alive right now, and it's a chance to see what we can do with this time.

SURVIVAL TIP

What you focus on ahead is the direction your life will go. It's true behind the wheel of your car and equally true behind the wheel of your life.

I now see that movement is an act of the body, but it must be given permission by the heart and soul. I made the choice to say "yes" to life even when I didn't know what I was saying. Somehow life accepted that as good enough and said "yes" back to me. It opened my heart through the love of some good people. It opened my mind to things that I could do. It opened my soul to the possibility of hope and goodness in the days ahead, even as the nights were the most empty and the days shrouded in fog. It showed me that I could laugh at myself and that sadness wasn't the only feeling in my vocabulary. It gave me permission to think about who I might be all by myself and how that might be enough to move forward. Life gave me hope and glimpses of how I could be a partner to it, as I started to create something new for myself. What it required from me was trust and the willingness to put out my hand and be open to what ended up in it. It also asked me to look for ways I could offer my hand and give something back. At first, the ways of returning the love were very small, but over time they are getting bigger. All in all, I'm encouraged. Maybe life can be good again, after all. What do you think?

Questions to ask as you move ahead with an open heart:

1. What gives you courage as you start moving forward?

2. What music opens your heart?

3. Who are the people you want around you? What roles do they play?

4. How will you live with yourself if or when you can't be the kind of friend to someone who has been so kind to you?

5. What words can you tell yourself that will move you forward?

A New Beginning

This book has been about "The Big Change," the one that knocks you to your knees because it's so unexpected. From my sixty-plus years of experience, including decades as a career counselor and life coach, I've seen life throw its knockout punches. It's terrifying to experience and heart-breaking to witness. "The Big Change" offers a gift, though. It's a chance to discover our core of steel, our outer limits of strength, our evidence of resiliency, and our talent for creating beauty. Smaller challenges, even if they once might have seemed big, are put into a new perspective. Nothing is ever the same, including our capacity to handle challenge. We're bigger, stronger, more sure that we will make it through because we already have. Van Morrison's "Down the Road," which I listened to over and over again, talks about "putting your soul back together." And I thought, that's it. I want my soul in one piece, whole and normal again. So, I sought a new beginning and wondered how I would know if life was listening to me.

These are such uncharted waters. And I'm still flying blind. Just when I think I've hit the last of the rapids, I go around a bend and get knocked out of the boat again. Lately I've been waking up with Terry's accident replaying over and over in my mind. Even if I shake it during the day, it catches up with me as I sleep. Damn. I want my nights back. I want to love spring again. I want to remember Terry's smile; the way he touched me when we made love; the way he used to make me laugh; the way he used to wander off, forcing me to use the cell phone to find him; and the pride I felt watching him lead another community meeting. When will the day and night come when those memories won't ache so much? I believe the day will come, but it's hard to be patient with the slow pace of this journey. It has a rhythm of its own, and even if I don't like it, I'm being forced to listen and to learn how to respect it.

I made it through the darkest nights of that first winter, waiting for the sweet gentleness of spring to help put me back together. Sometimes the days felt even longer, and I still ached with the emptiness of a life that once was so full. I was coming of age in my sixties and thinking, "What a fine time to discover who I really am." Would there really be enough time? Will the mind hold on? Will the body? Will one part spring a leak and take down the whole ship before the new adventure gets going? Oh, the questions and the sense of urgency.

I remember I was perched on the kitchen counter watching Terry cook dinner and sipping a glass of Shiraz months before he died when we started talking about his businesses. I jokingly told him that I needed to die first, because there was no way I could manage them. Then life showed something else in store. The learning curve was as steep as a Mount Rainier slope, and there was no time to get in shape. The minute he died, his businesses were mine and it felt like I was on the mountain way too soon.

So, when does the new beginning *really* begin? How will we know that the tide has really turned? The calendar obviously doesn't determine it. I think it happens by design, by intent, by trusting, by the weight of one brave act piled onto another, and by willingness to be courageous when that is the last thing we think we are capable of. And it doesn't happen alone. It takes a community of willing hands to carry us over the threshold. The pieces of me that fell away when Terry died surely didn't all die with him. Some remained to help me discover the woman I was about to become.

I believe that new beginnings start with the belief in the right to take a big step, then doing it. I remember years ago hiking with a team of eleven other women. Picture us huddled on a rock ledge 140 feet above a hard granite base at the top of Twin Peak in the rugged Sierra Nevada Mountains in California. A looming thunderstorm finally gave me the courage to overcome my paralyzing fear, grab my ropes, and step over the edge into a perfect rappel. Haven't we heard that the first step is the hardest? Well, it's true. The first step in scooping up the shattered bits of a life and daring to create a new reality is to gather information from every angle, including from 14,000 feet up. It is in asking the tough questions, taking the time to get some perspective, and then writing down the answers. It ultimately lays a strong foundation for a brighter future.

In my case, days spent gathering pictures from magazines yielded a collage filled with pictures bright with hope and possibility. It spoke to me of my beginnings in California, of my life with Terry, and of the curiosity that would open doors to a yet-to-be-discovered future. At dead center was a photograph of a crevasse that spoke of the emotional chasm I would have to cross in order to find the bright future that was pictured with such beauty. Somehow my intuition found just the right pictures to keep me honest and to also give me hope.

I also found inspiration in a series of exercises in Helen Harkness' *Don't Stop the Career Clock.* Her questions are really meant for people thinking about retirement, but I think they work for any big life change. I completed the life-cycle chart and assessed my personal needs and accomplishments. A picture was forming. It was familiar in some ways and new in others. I felt both reassured and at times surprised.

At the same time that I hungered for information, my own aliveness called me to action. My accomplice in that first call sits in the garage surrounded by chunks of bark: an eighty-pound, hydraulic, DR® four-ton wood splitter I ordered online. It yielded beautiful, split firewood from trees that I had to take down for safety and to help make happy neighbors, both at work and at home. I handled every piece of that cord and a half, most of it more than once, and all by myself. How satisfying. I loved the sound the logs made when they split and now the smell of the garage when I come home from work. I love looking at the pile of log rounds getting smaller and the split stack growing fatter. Because the last thing Terry did for me was to have a fireplace installed in our bedroom, these logs burn brightly in it on the dark nights when he can't be there himself to warm me. They symbolize a new start.

My beautiful red car has also been a symbol. A car makes a statement about our spirit, our desires, and our degree of willingness to be noticed in the world. Friends and family teased me about police supposedly giving out more speeding tickets to drivers of red cars. They also joked about my car "being a dude magnet." When friends asked the name of the car, I paused. A name is a serious responsibility, and I didn't want to just toss out an answer. One morning, though, her name arrived in the wisp of a dream: Annie. It comes from the "Ann" part of my name, the fact that Terry would call me "Annie" when he was feeling playful, and from the redhead Little Orphan Annie in one of my favorite Broadway plays. I wanted the name to be lively, fun, and full of spirit. That's also how I want to feel when I drive her.

That feeling of being alive with clarity of purpose is at the core of creating our new lives. Are we here just to draw one breath after another until we die? Or are we here for some grander purpose? Clues to my answer kept coming from the daily life choices I made. I found myself making sure the house was filled with flowers. I made a commitment to support our local farmers market and was faithful in going every Saturday I was in town. I worked in the yard to help make it beautiful. I continued to take photographs and to bake birthday cakes from scratch for people I love. I looked for ways to build people up and tell them about it. When friends asked for help or support, I'd try to say, "I'm in." And I gave money to other causes that needed that kind of support. If I could put my heart, my time, or my money behind something important, I looked for what that said about me. Ultimately, I am hoping that will allow me to be more alive, more aware, more deliberate, more conscious, and much more directed with who I am and what I do.

This challenge of rebuilding our lives after sudden loss also can be inspired by personal creativity. If we can bake a birthday cake from scratch, build a house, or plant a vegetable garden, what does that say about the way we might build a life? Often when I work with clients, we talk about *how* they accomplish a task, whether it is designing a bridge, teaching a class, or writing a résumé. As they talk, I write down the steps they take to move from the idea to the accomplishment. The way each person creates is unique. Instead of reinventing the wheel, I look for how the person gets a job done. For *me* to be creative, I have to have a vision of what I want in my head. All my tools have to be sharp and ready. I begin with a mind map to organize my ideas and capture them into some kind of whole. And then I begin.

Another tool I use with clients is the SMART criteria, given to me by a friend long ago. It helps us determine if an idea is just a dream or a real goal through a series of five questions: 1. Am I **S**incere about this idea? Do I have the passion to sustain it when the end point is still far away? 2. Is it **M**easurable? How will I know that I have accomplished my goal? 3. Is it **A**vailable? Is it within my world? 4. Is it **R**ealistic to be working on this idea? 5. And is the **T**iming right? In every case, we are looking for the word "yes." Anything less than "yes" means the idea really isn't ready to be a goal.

One of my dreams was to be in relationship again. For the longest time, the only criteria I could answer with "yes" was, "Is it measurable?" Obviously that idea was still a distant dream and nowhere near being a goal. Then one day a friend asked if I was willing to go to coffee with one of her husband's friends, a widower. At first I recoiled, but after a month of thinking it over, I finally was able to say "yes" to the five criteria and agreed to get together. When he called, it was obvious that he was as nervous as I was, and that made it somehow easier. We met for coffee and it was fun. The time flew by, and I enjoyed his stories, his energy, and his passion for life. Later he joked about how much he had talked and how little I had. Eventually it seemed to me that he was still very much grieving the loss of his wife and soulmate, and he said goodbye. Goodbye is a big word in my vocabulary now, but he used it well and honestly. For that I will be forever grateful.

Making new connections feels very much like a bridge to the future, and these days it's all about finding ways to link up with possible friends and potential mates in our high-octane, everyone's-wired world. The casual talk at a creativity class I took was about "speed dating," where the goal is to rip through conversations, weeding out those people we aren't interested in so we can find the few we might like to know better. My last issue of the AARP magazine had a lengthy article on the value of using services such as Match.com or eHarmony.com to do the same thing. So I tried Match.com. I immediately found it's not for sissies. I had to be willing to take a bunch of tests and write about who I am and the kind of person I want to meet. Then the computer told me I was picky. Well, fine. Next I learned about "winks" indicating interest, and how many times people looked at my site. At one point I had 350-plus viewings and only seven winks. So I had questions: Was I too old? Was I too weird in my ideas? Maybe I didn't stack up. Maybe I'd better make peace with being single the rest of my life. I didn't want that to be a goal. I wanted to be able to be whole in who I am, enough for what I can create out of the possibilities of my own unique qualities.

And healing comes in different forms. The other night I had a dream about Terry, only the second one I've had about him since he died. He was walking in the back door after work just as he always did, only this time he was carrying a large, half-eaten combination pizza. He was holding it up like a banquet waiter carrying a tray full of plates. He called out to me, "Honey, I'm home!" I started to reach for him when the thought crossed my dreaming mind that I had already eaten dinner. How was I going to eat a second dinner when I was already full? Then in my dream I looked at him and thought, "How can you be here when you are dead?" The dream was so vivid that it woke me up thinking, "I get it that you really are gone." And then I realized, I am taking care of myself now. We're done with what was ours to share, and I am feeding myself now.

The next day was misty, one of those Northwest days that finally felt familiar after such a glorious, sun-filled summer. I lit a fire in my bedroom fireplace using wood that I had split, and I began planning what it would take to make Dixie's birthday cake the next day. Then it hit me for a fleeting second. I felt happy. In my heart I was aware that I was beginning to create and live a life that had meaning to me in those small ways that feed me. It was the most amazing feeling to know that I could be happy with the life I was building. It was hope, trust in myself, and confidence in life itself that had finally floated up to the surface of my awareness. I wasn't sure life would ever be hopeful again, and yet here it was.

Somehow, if I could bake a cake to celebrate someone I loved, maybe the world wasn't going to end after all. My world crashed when Terry died, but I finally am realizing that as hard as it has been, I can live a good life. I have built a strong foundation, and as I face the future, it is with hope and confidence.

What I've learned about grief and rebuilding a life after sudden loss:

1. The experience has a life of its own.

2. It's universal and also very personal.

3. Going through it is hard and necessary.

4. Don't be afraid to cry, even in public.

5. The love is as deep as the pain.

6. It's not something to do alone.

7. It's possible to laugh even in the middle of the deepest pain.

8. Animals are a great source of comfort.

9. It's OK to eat peanut butter from a spoon for dinner, as long as it's not permanent.

10. Friends will do the most amazing and generous things.

11. Trusting yourself is an act of courage.

12. Getting through takes a village.

13. Not everyone is nice, and that's a fact.

14. Really good "paid friends" make a difference.

15. Taking action where the results are immediate and can be seen pays big returns.

16. Taking care of your car helps.

17. Planting bulbs in the fall proves winter doesn't last forever, and we can still make beautiful things happen.

18. Giving the gift of life by being an organ donor feels great.

19. Romance novels are worth the money.

20. It's worth asking the hard questions and trusting that the answers will come.

From Surviving to Thriving: A Postscript

It's been seven years now since Terry died. I still think of him when I look over the waters of the Puget Sound from our property, especially when I see a trawler go by. One of his dreams was to own a forty-two-foot Grandbanks, a fancy trawler, and I've actually seen a few on the water. They are so sturdy and look so safe in the water. I think of him when I still see our sprinkler heads held up by screwdrivers—he must have gotten a deal on them. I think of him when I hear certain songs, especially on my iPod. He would have loved all the new toys and advances in technology. And I think of him when I stand in the kitchen and cook dinner at the same place where he cooked so many delicious meals. He'd be pleased that I have rediscovered cooking. It was one of his favorite ways to celebrate, and now one of mine, too.

Terry is still part of the fabric of my life, but my life has gone on in new ways that don't belong to him. I found a wonderful new man on Match.com, my Dr. Jim, to laugh with and to love. He's filled with kindness and acceptance, with interests and experiences that pique my curiosity. His large and love-filled family has been generous in its willingness to take me in. He's a dairy expert and consultant, so you can now ask me a thing or two about Holsteins and Jerseys. He's a big baseball fan, so I started knitting again in order to "watch" games with him on TV. He loves birds, so we spend part of our time watching them, and I find it both fun and peaceful. He's a wonderful grandpa to Ben and to our newest and most beautiful granddaughter, Grace. Ben recently made his first solo trip to our home to spend some time with us, and Grandpa Jim kept him busy around the clock. Jim used his talent and skill with animals to find us a beautiful orange-and- white cat named Tigger at the humane society after Bogey and Katey passed on. Tigger is definitely living the good life now. Lucky guy!

I'm still active in the community, and Jim and I took advantage of a funding campaign for our new library to make a contribution in honor of Terry, the Terry D. Reim Spirit of University Place Donor Wall. We can hardly wait to see it. I still hold Terry's original seat on the economic development commission, but I can see at some point that I will want to let someone else have my place at the table. Fresh ideas from new people are good.

I've rediscovered my artistic interests, having taken up knitting again after forty years, as I mentioned before. It is like riding a bicycle—the movements are rusty at first but eventually return. I've made everyone I know scarves, and I've also made a couple of vests and the cutest hats and sweaters for Grace. I've also resumed work on a watercolor wall quilt for Brandon that had been on hold since Terry died. I can hardly wait to see how it turns out. And, finally, I discovered how much I love writing. It is the most wonderful discovery of all.

Passion for life fills my days now. Courageous clients continue to find me, and we work together to help them create the kinds of lives they want. Jim and I planted a vegetable garden that seems to be responding to the word "grow" on a sign we nailed over the garden gate. We surrounded the garden with an eight-foot-high fence to encourage Bambi and her deer family to stay on the outside, and it's working. I am in love with that garden and am thrilled as I see the tiny plants and seeds become delicious beans, lettuce, and tomatoes that we share and pick for dinner.

I have found warmth again inside my own heart. It is the gift of life. Finally I can feel it again. Life and all its warmth waited for me, and I know it is waiting for you, too.

Ackowledgments and Thanks

The following extraordinary people deserve a huge thank you. My two children, Tracey and Brandon, have shown themselves to be made of gold. Without their support, encouragement, time, love, talents, and senses of humor, I would just now be beginning to rebuild. I love them so much. Also, I want to give big hugs to my son-in-law, Steve, who is the best in the world. He is amazing in his support and counsel. My grandson, Ben, who is the Prince of Summit and who uttered those magic words, "I love you, Grandma," can have anything he ever wants. His little sister, Grace, is the frosting on the cupcake. She is twinkle and beauty in a tiny body. One look and I was hers. Thank you to cousin Candy, who dropped everything when Terry died and was at my side before even one day had passed. You are amazing. Thank you to my mom, who was a star as she faced her own mountains to climb. She climbed them with grace and humor and was truly a role model. Thank you to Terry's sister Darla and her husband, George, who continue to consider me family and whose love is as warm as the Oklahoma sun. Thank you as well to Mom and Dad Reim, who have been generous with their patience and have continued to call me even when I sometimes forget to check my voice mail. Thanks to Uncle Milton, who fielded a number of tearful phone calls from me, even as he was facing the loss of Aunt Bobbi and was dealing with his own grief.

I also have a family of friends who have given me the gifts of their love, time, talent, counsel, and wisdom over and over. I promise to pay it forward for the rest of my life. To Margaret Ann, sister of my heart, and her soulmate, Art, your gentle love, humor, and beautiful flowers have been part of my bridge to new life. You are incredible. Nancy, out of everyone I know, you are the one who could tell me that Terry is doing really well where he is. Your gift is priceless and so are you. I love you so much. To Pat and Glee, there are so many ways that you have become the family of my heart. From your willingness, Glee, to drive my way at 6:30 in the morning to walk, to helping me with my depression after our fortieth wedding anniversary, to including me in your family holidays, you are in my heart forever. Pat, your wise counsel on the business challenges I faced almost immediately has been the steadying force in my life. What is that old ad line, "When E.F. Hutton speaks, everyone listens"? Well, when you speak, I listen, and your wisdom has always been on the mark! To Dixie, you are like my younger sister, and I know that you were Terry's soulmate. You make the best birthday cakes and really know how to throw a party. Not only that, but you have the courage to step into the hardest situations and not waver an inch. To Bud, you are the best driving teacher. Thanks for not laughing at me too much when I shifted in the middle of a turn. When we talk about friends, Gary and Jan are the best and the kindest. Sitting around your dining room table and being part of your family, laughing and crying with you through the years has formed a bond that will never break. Bill and Sue are my family across the blue waters of the Pacific. You are my brother, Bill, and it's because of you that Terry found the most beautiful place on earth to rest while he waits for all of us to join him. You brought us the magic of Kauai and continue to bring me the gifts of laughter and connection. Sue, you are just beauty personified, and whenever you are around I feel better. Lis, somehow you knew what I needed when Terry died, and I was walking around in a haze. Not only that, but your gift of asking me to join you in the Women of Courage group was absolutely amazing. I loved it and I love you. Dyann and Bill, you are my role models. Dyann, your beauty and courage as you walked your own difficult passage lighted the way for me. What an extraordinary woman you are. Patrick, over and over you have taken me to lunch, first accompanied by tears and now by laughter. What a brave man. To the women in my office, thank you for holding me, laughing and crying with me, and for saying, "You go girl. We're behind you!"

Finally, there are three people without whom this book would not have happened. First is my husband, Dr. Jim, who has been my cheerleader, patient friend, and helpmate as this book evolved from its original version. He is such an amazing man. Next is Colleen, who said, "I can help you," and did. Finally is our most extraordinary editor, Doreen. It has been a labor of love working with her. She is such a bright star, and I am so grateful for her love and talent in making this book the best it can be. I love you all.

About the Author

Ruthann Reim McCaffree (www.CareerMI.com) has been a life coach, counselor and change management consultant to such companies as AT&T, Weyerhauser, Russell Investments and The News Tribune since 1984. She founded the Career Management Institute in 1989 and has coached and counseled thousands of individuals in managing their lives effectively. She lives in University Place, Washington with her husband, Jim, and two cats.